ROBOTICS
Past, Present, & Future

ROBOTICS
Past, Present, & Future
By DAVID C. KNIGHT

ILLUSTRATED WITH PHOTOGRAPHS

William Morrow & Company • New York / 1983

TITLE PAGE: Moviegoers of the 1950s were captivated by the antics of friendly, helpful Robby the Robot in the MGM film *Forbidden Planet*. To many he still epitomizes the man-machine.

PAGE VI: Two popular movie robots of the late 1970s film *Star Wars* were the rather elegant humanoid type, C-3PO (left), and his dome-headed companion, R2-D2, a worker type.

PICTURE CREDITS: Museum of Modern Art/Film Stills Archive, pp. iii, 11, 55; Lucasfilm Ltd., p. VI; Scantrak Corp., pp. 5,117,120; Cincinnati Milacron, pp. 7, 75, 76; Unimation, Inc., pp. 13, 50, 70, 73; German National Tourist Bureau, p. 22; Musée d'Art et d'Histoire, Neuchâtel, Switzerland, p. 25; The Franklin Institute, pp. 27, 29; Sperry Rand Corp., p. 47; Prab Robots, Inc., p. 51; Massachusetts Institute of Technology, p. 53; General Electric Co., p. 65; Raytheon Corp., pp. 77, 83; Hughes Aircraft Co., p. 80; Bell Telephone Laboratories, p. 98; Veterans Administration, p. 103; National Aeronautics and Space Administration, p. 108; United Press International, p. 114.

2   3   4   5   6   7   8   9   10
Library of Congress Cataloging in Publication Data
Knight, David C.   Robotics, past, present, and future.
Includes index. Summary: Discusses the history and workings of robots and automata; their many uses in industry, homes, offices, medicine, and space; and their possible future applications.
1. Automata—Juvenile literature. [1. Automata. 2. Robots] I. Title.
TJ211.K58   1983   629.8'92   82-22918
ISBN 0-688-01490-9

Contents

ONE

What Is a Robot?

From earliest times people have been tantalized by a persistent dream: if artificial people could be constructed in the human image and made to perform useful work, men and women could be freed from backbreaking and often tedious labor. Liberated, they could enjoy unlimited leisure to pursue more rewarding activities.

The word that springs to most peoples' minds for such helpful mechanical creatures is *robot*. It was coined by the Czechoslovakian dramatist

ROBOTICS

Karel Čapek in his 1921 play called *R.U.R.* The play was about artificial men, and Čapek took the name from the Czech word *robota*, which means "compulsory service" or "work." So popular was *R.U.R.* in Europe and America that *robot* stuck in peoples' minds as standing for any mechanical man possessing human characteristics, and the word entered most of the world's languages.

In *R.U.R.*—whose initials stand for Rossum's Universal Robots—mechanical men devoid of human frailties and emotions are turned out at Rossum's factory in vast numbers to do the world's work. Docile and obedient, the robots toil away in factories and elsewhere, never complaining, never tiring, never making mistakes. The robots' creators, seeking a way to make them work harder and more efficiently, hit on the idea of endowing them with human emotions such as love and hate. However, instead of making the robots work better, the emotions have the effect of making them rebellious and unruly. In the end, the robots stage a global revolt, eradicate their human creators, and assume command of the world.

While the robots in Čapek's play were, of course, actors dressed up as metallic artificial

2

A scene from the first New York production of Čapek's *R.U.R.* in 1922. Radius, one of Rossum's Universal Robots, confronts the woman, Helen.

men, machines that are also called robots are very much a part of our world today. A robot differs from an ordinary machine in that it is an automatic device that performs functions usually thought of as human. That is, it operates with seemingly human intelligence. A robot can further be described as an automatic machine that does the work, or part of the work, of human beings when it is activated by radio, light, or sound waves, by electronic impulses, or by some other form of energy. Also in general usage today is the term *robotic device,* which refers to a machine having the characteristics of a robot; both are often used interchangeably.

The term *automaton* is sometimes incorrectly used to mean a robot or robotic device. The word comes from the Greek *automatos,* which means "self-acting." An automaton is a machine, often in human form, incorporating mechanisms that perform without human intervention. A toy doll that, when wound up and released, can walk across the floor is an automaton. In other words, an automaton is a self-moving machine, one often constructed to imitate the actions of men, birds, and animals. Another important distinction between an automaton and a robot is that the energy source of the automaton is limited; for example, a toy doll's windup mechanism eventually runs down and must be wound up again. The automatons fashioned by the master craftsmen of the eighteenth and nineteenth century were heralds of today's robots. Occasionally the term *android* (meaning "man-form" from its Greek roots *andros* and *eidos*) is used to mean robot; how-

4

A typical display robot, or showbot. Standing about five feet tall with fiber-glass bodies and plastic head and arm covers, these "mechanical humanoids" can roll about and even speak on radio command.

ever, it occurs mainly in science-fiction stories.

The robots we see about us today come in many shapes and sizes. Some of these are constructed in human form, with metal or plastic heads, arms, and legs. The simplest of these are mechanical toys that can move about on wheels or mechanical legs and even "talk." Were these mere windup toys, they would be classified as automatons, but most operate on batteries and are frequently radio-controlled. Commands are given to them via a hand-held radio signal unit. More complicated humanoid-type robots are those built for display, publicity, or entertainment. These also operate by radio control. There are experimental robots that can play chess, draw pictures, play the piano, and perform other functions. A series of small motors built into these robots respond to radio signals transmitted by an operator, who can program them to carry out the desired function.

Still other robots bear no similarity to human beings at all. Some, such as a pacemaker that monitors and regulates a patient's heartbeat, can be held in the palm of one's hand. Others, such as a network of computers that automatically operates an oil refinery, are obviously huge. There are devices in our homes that we may not recognize as robots. But robots they are because they do chores for us in an automatic fashion. These include thermostats that turn furnaces and air conditioners on and off, machines programed to wash our clothes, microwave ovens adjusted to cook our food in a certain length of time, and dozens of others. In our factories, there are highly complex machines called "industrial robots" that perform specific work tasks such as welding and handling of goods and materials. In addition, there are specialized robotic devices that pilot high-speed planes and guided missiles, mine coal, report the weather, act as prosthetic devices, steer ocean liners, and carry out a host of other automatic operations.

This T-3 industrial robot is shown welding a base assembly for a computer main frame. It can weld forty-four two-inch seams from a variety of angles in under twelve minutes. It took a human worker nearly an hour to weld the same frame.

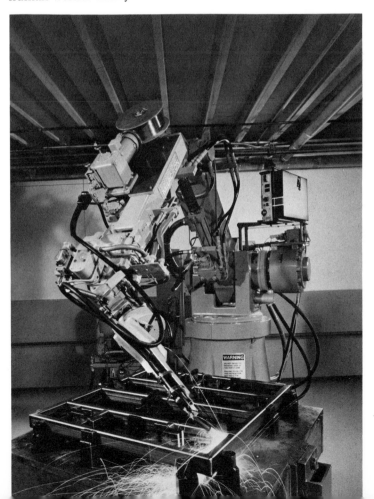

ROBOTICS

As indispensable as robots have become to our modern civilization, certain fears and suspicions have grown up about them during what might be termed their social history. These still persist today in some peoples' minds. In some countries robots are feared as stealers of jobs. Or the robot is often imagined as a mechanical monster whose malevolent brain is intent on the destruction of human kind. The stigma attached to robots has largely been inspired by modern stories, books, and films about robots.

In literature, robots acquired an early sinister reputation. As early as 1910, the American author Ambrose Bierce published a story called "Moxon's Master," in which a robot chess-player strangles to death a human opponent who has beat it in a match. A few years later, a film featuring an evil robot and loosely based on Gustav Meyrink's novel *The Golem* was being shown in Europe. In these early decades of the twentieth century, works of science fiction perpetuated the idea of the wickedness of mechanical creatures. In France, Romaine Rolland wrote *The Revolt of the Machines* and Georges Bernanos, *France Against the Robots*. In England, E. M. Forster depicted superhuman

man-machines in "The Machine Stops," while H. G. Wells hinted darkly of possible machine supremacy in *The Shape of Things to Come.*

In America, L. Frank Baum wrote *The Tik-Tok Man of Oz;* its protagonist was a mechanical automaton which, when wound up, always did what it was told—sometimes at the expense of humans. In the 1930s, the science-fiction writer Eando Binder wrote his forty famous robot stories, to be followed a few years later by Isaac Asimov's popular novel, *I, Robot.* Meanwhile, science-fiction magazines such as *Galaxy* and *Fantastic Universe* were churning out tales of races of masterful robots pitted against human beings. Frequently these stories harped on the theme that human beings are growing "soft" and decadent because machines are doing all the work for them; hence, robot take-over of society must be inevitable.

In 1926, taking advantage of the public fancy for robots kindled by *R.U.R.* and other works, the director Fritz Lang brought robots to the screen in *Metropolis.* The picture's chief character is a female robot named Maria, whose creator—the classic mad scientist—intends her to go forth in the world on evangelical missions. Instead, Maria

A representative science-fiction magazine cover of the 1940s and 1950s, depicting metal humanoid robots in human situations.

goes berserk, incites workers to riot, and nearly causes great damage as she tries to destroy humanity.

The revolutionary robots of *R.U.R.* and *Metropolis,* coming as they did on the heels of World War I and the social unrest that followed it, did little to promote the image of robots as benefactors in the future. Neither did the scary robot science fiction being written. Rather, these works tended to crystalize the distrust many people had of machines as they developed rapidly through the 1930s and

1940s. Even those who scoffed at the notion of robot take-over as nonsense found the idea of superefficient automatic machines vaguely disturbing. Might not robots take away peoples' jobs? The future seemed too precious to entrust to such machines.

Not surprisingly in a society so conditioned, the first industrial robots were regarded with suspi-

A production scene from the film *Metropolis*. Fritz Lang, the director (at left), adjusts attitude and lighting of the woman robot, Maria.

cion and dismay when they went on assembly lines in the late 1950s. When some workers did lose their jobs, irate labor unions tried to block the use of machines. One outcome of this controversy was that in 1962, organized labor was able to get management to agree that industrial robots would be made to pay union dues. Accordingly, as each new industrial robot began its job in various plants in the United States, it—or rather its owners— had to pay from $25 to $1000 a year, depending on how many man-hours the robot worked and what kind of job it performed. These robots' dues went into a general fund for studying the problem of human workers and automation. For robots themselves were helping to bring about increased automation by staffing factories and turning out products automatically. Obviously the robots were here to stay and, as one scientist put it, a new kind of integration problem was upon us—the integration of human beings and machines.

Today the problem of "technological unemployment" still exists. While robots—particularly industrial robots—serve us each day, often performing tasks we could never hope to on our own, we would be shortsighted to ignore the serious prob-

An industrial robot at work. This Unimate, after extracting a part from a die-casting machine, immerses it in a quench tank.

lems they have engendered. The unhappy fact is that, as more robots come into use, people will continue to be eased out of certain jobs. However, it is also a fact that those jobs—often taxing, uncomfortable, and boring ones—are the least desirable for any human being to perform. Furthermore, many companies both here and abroad make it a policy to retrain for other jobs people who have been replaced by a robotic device.

13

ROBOTICS

On the positive side, there is the bright hope that the integration of human beings and machines can eventually be accomplished, with the machines themselves helping to solve the problems they have created. With our businesses and industries becoming ever more complex, we desperately need robots to cope with the volume of work to be done. Without them, in a technological civilization fairly bursting at the seams, only a fraction of that work could be accomplished. Because the electrical and mechanical controls of robots are more accurate than the human hand or eye, many of the products robotically produced are better made. Because robots are faster than people, production of goods is increased, and in many cases, this increase lessens their cost. At the same time, in automated industries using robots, the work week has been shortened and people are left with more leisure time. This change has already taken place in Japan.

Yet automation remains controversial. People who are enthusiastic about it point out that every step in the improvement of machines has put some people out of work but that in the long run there has been an increase in the total number of jobs. To some extent they are right, for there is now a greater need than ever for scientists, engineers, and skilled technicians to design more automated machines and to keep them running. Critics point out there is no guarantee this need will always exist, however, and that, even if automation does create new jobs, it will still take time for these new jobs to develop for the unskilled laborers who have been replaced. In the meantime, many people may suffer, through no fault of their own, until the number of new jobs catches up with the number of displaced workers.

In any case, since robots are here to stay, the technology that has given rise to them has spawned a new science. Called "robotics," it is involved with the design, application, and maintenance of the whole range of robotic devices. Those who work in robotics firmly believe that their machines, used intelligently and imaginatively, are not our foes but our faithful servants—just as Rossum of *R.U.R.* intended them to be.

TWO

Origins and History

Most people tend to think of robots as products of our modern machine age. However, the notion of creating artificial creatures with the capabilities of human beings and animals goes back for thousands of years. Robots in human form, for example, appeared in Greek mythology. In Homer's *Iliad,* a bronze mechanical man guarded the island of Crete for King Minos. And Daedalus, the mythical Greek artisan who flew with artificial wings, was said to have made working models of

16

gods. One, a wooden replica of the goddess Venus, could move its arms in a remarkably lifelike manner.

Centuries before these myths developed, the ancient Egyptians were building simple robot figures that imitated animal and human functions. In a tomb dating from about 2000 B.C., a graceful sculpture of a dog was found. When a lever in its stomach is pressed, the dog's mouth opens. In the Louvre Museum in Paris there is a painted wooden figure of an Egyptian baker. His arms move and in his hands he holds a stone, with which he can be made to pound grain into flour. Pegs join his arms to his shoulder sockets. The pegs act as fulcrums, or turning points, for the arms, which are actually levers. When a counterweight behind the figure and attached to the arms is slid back or forth, the arms move up or down. Crude though it is, the figure shows that its creator understood how the mechanics of human joints work—certainly a first important step toward the manufacture of a manlike machine.

In the first century B.C., the Greek inventor Hero of Alexandria constructed a robotic device that could open and close temple doors. It was actually a rudimentary example of a power train (commonly employed today in mechanisms such as cars) in which one action triggers another, then another, and so on until a desired action is accomplished. As shown in the diagram, a fire near the doors caused the air in a container underneath the doors to expand, forcing water into a pail. The weight of the water caused the pail to descend on a rope system. As it did so, the pail pulled other ropes attached to turning rollers that opened the temple doors. When the fire was extinguished, the air contracted, sucking the water

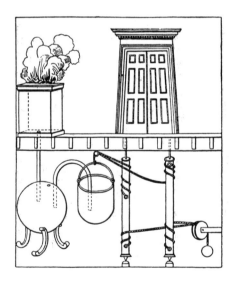

A robotic device by the early Greek inventor Hero of Alexandria, used for opening and closing temple doors.

back into the container. A counterweight closed the doors again.

During the Middle Ages, the automatons began to appear. Built in the shapes of birds, animals, and people, they were heralds of the machine age and modern robots. Capable of performing complete sequences of motions, they derived their motive power from the mechanisms of clocks. Many were connected to the large clockwork on town halls, churches, and state buildings. Some automatons could perform human work, such as pouring water and ringing bells. Their complex mechanisms were the creation of master craftsmen who combined the talents of engineer, sculptor, armorer, and metalsmith. The trip levers, springs, gears, and rods that caused them to move could extend some distance from their clockwork power source, giving the illusion that they moved all by themselves.

One of the most famous of these automatons is the rooster perched atop the great cathedral at Strasbourg in France. As it has since the year 1350, each day at noon the rooster flaps its wings, thrusts out its tongue, and crows. The intricacy of its mechanism can be appreciated in the diagram on page 21. A sliding, turning rod in each leg of the fowl is connected by a train of gears to the work of the cathedral clock. Each of these main rods is connected to several series of other rod-systems inside the body of the rooster. These internal rod-systems are coupled together by universal joints, which permit swiveling and turning at any angle. One system causes the wings to flap, another makes the bird thrust out its tongue, and so forth. The two main leg rods, preprogrammed to twist, turn, raise, and lower at certain intervals, activate the several internal rod systems, which then carry out the mechanical rooster's various functions.

The celebrated German *glockenspiels*—"players of the bells"—were also automatons connected to clockwork. Perhaps the most elaborate glockenspiel is the one on the main spire of Nuremberg's Frauenkirche. In a grand processional display, a whole band of figures, walking, playing instruments, and ringing bells, sound out the hours. Actually an immense music box, it has programming devices that are basically the same as those of all other clockwork automatons, only this one is conceived on a much grander scale. In a motion typical of all of the figures, a cherub

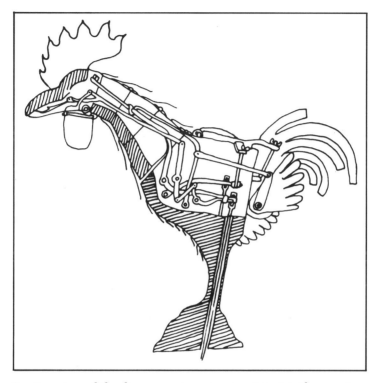

Section view of the famous automaton rooster atop the great cathedral of Strasbourg in France.

raises and lowers his trumpet with one of his arms. A cam system, drawing its power from the main clockwork, is responsible for the motion. The cherub's arm is nothing more than a lever pivoted at the figure's shoulder socket with a metal pin which allows the arm holding the trumpet to

21

The elaborate *Glockenspiel* on the main spire of Nuremberg's Frauenkirche features an array of performing automatons.

move up and down. Concealed from the public under the arm at the bicep area is the slowly rotating heart-cam wheel, drawing its motion from the gear wheels of the clockwork. This heart-cam is a wheel that bulges at one of its edges. When the bulge of the cam, underneath the arm and always in contact with it, reaches its highest point, it pushes the arm with it. The arm then lowers by its own weight as the narrow edge of the cam wheel allows it to do so.

By the mid-eighteenth century with the Industrial Revolution moving into full swing, new tools, new machines, and new sources of power rendered it possible to devise mechanisms that could, within limited spaces, control whole sequences of motions and actions. Craftsmen fascinated with simulating real-life actions could now create new and more complex automatons. One of the most famous of these was a highly intricate mechanical duck constructed by the French inventor Jacques de Vaucanson. The duck could flap its wings, quack, drink, bathe, walk, and appear to eat food. It actually operated by a weight-driven mechanism housed in the large base upon which it was exhibited. The duck was made to walk by means of a rotating axle rod, to which were attached two half-gear wheels. These half gears were exactly that—180 degrees of a geared wheel instead of a full 360 degree geared wheel. They were like a coin cut in half. These two half-geared wheels, themselves out of phase with each other by 180 degrees, were made to mesh with gear teeth projecting upward from the duck's feet which could move back and forth. First one half-geared wheel would engage the teeth on one foot of the duck, then the other would engage the teeth on the other foot. If the half gears had been normal, whole circular gears, the walking could not have taken place. But with the alternate action of the half gears, the mechanical duck could put one foot in front of the other and walk.

Some of the most exquisite automatons ever made were those of the eighteenth-century inventor Pierre Jacquet-Droz. Three of these clockwork-driven figures can be seen in operation today at the Fine Arts Museum in Neuchâtel, Switzerland. Each is about three feet tall. One, a lady artist, draws pictures with grand flourishes. Another, a boy, dips his pen into an inkwell and writes whatever short message the operator selects. A

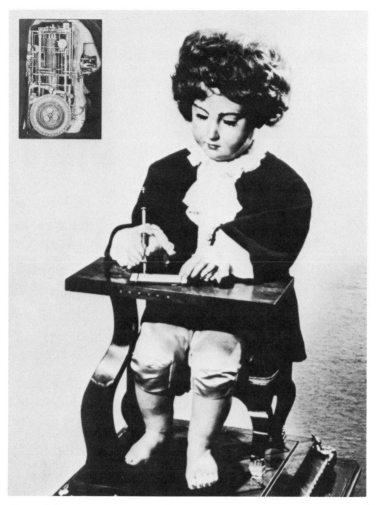

One of the most exquisite of Pierre Jacquet-Droz's eighteenth-century automatons. The clockwork-driven figure dips his pen in an inkwell and writes whatever short message the operator selects.

third figure, a lady musician, plays upon a spinet with all ten fingers.

Jacquet-Droz had a pupil who was every bit as gifted as he. He was Henri Maillardet, and he created and exhibited several ingenious automatons. One of them, known as the Maillardet Automaton, can be seen in Philadelphia's Franklin Institute. This seated female figure both writes in fancy penmanship and sketches pictures. Her body is made of strips of brass and wire, and the glass floor upon which her chair rests reveals the spring-driven motor that operates her.

The Maillardet Automaton works in the same way as Jacquet-Droz's figures. Essentially, the spring motor causes the rotation of a central axle upon which are mounted three separate sections of cam wheels. The ridges or "lumps" on the edges of each of these wheels represent a movement that will result in an individual letter of the alphabet being written by the automaton's hand. As the diagram shows, there is a follower arm above each section of cam wheels. Each of the three arms is mounted on a common axle rod and moves easily up and down. The free end of each arm rests lightly upon a delicate bar, mounted in

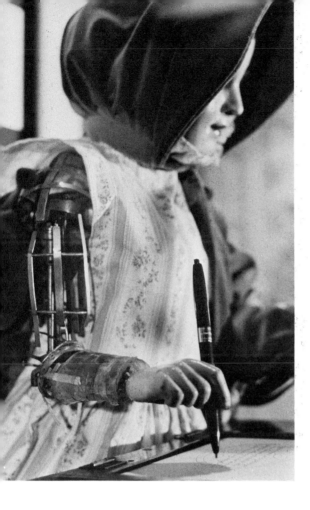

The Maillardet Automaton as it is usually displayed at the Franklin Institute in Philadelphia. Operated by a spring-driven motor, the seated female figure both writes and sketches pictures.

such a way that it rides on top of the cam wheels and picks up their individual undulations.

As the cam wheels revolve, the "lumps" on their edges cause the delicate bar to be pushed up and down in certain positions. The follower arms, which can slide back and forth laterally along the bars, pick up the individual cam wheel motions and transmit them to a mechanical system inside the automaton's body. This system, an intricate network of rods, levers, and shafts, carries the cam motions up the body, across the shoulders, and down to the writing arm, whose hand holds a pen resting on a sheet of paper. If, for example, the writing arm receives a cam motion for the letter C, it writes that character. If the next cam motion denotes A, the hand writes an A. If the third is for T, the arm translates that motion into a written T on the paper. Hence, the automaton has written CAT. Actually, the lady does not write CAT but is pre-set by its human operator to perform a limited number of programmed motions, such as sketching a picture of a ship or writing a short message (see the accompanying illustrations). Before this automaton was brought to America, it and several others were the star attractions at the Haymarket Exhibition in London in 1825.

The long heyday of the automatons lasted from the late 1700s right through the nineteenth century. People flocked to exhibitions to wach them perform their measured, intricate movements. One major obstacle that confronted the automaton makers was speech. Without speech, the artificial "humans" were less than convincing. Inventors racked their brains, trying everything they could think of to make their automatons talk or sing. They used vibrating reeds, diaphragms in tiny voice boxes, and even bellows to blow air into complex whistles. One Turkish lady automaton on

Left, diagram showing the operation of the Maillardet Automaton. Right, sketches and writing produced by the figure.

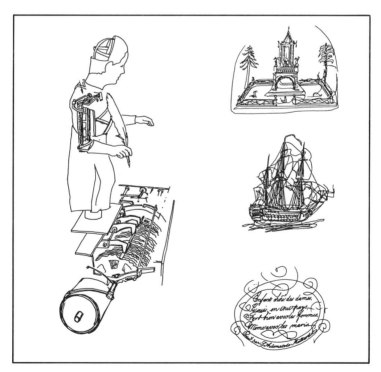

exhibit in Paris could make voicelike noises through a trumpet attached to her lips. Using a leather squeeze bulb and hose, her operator forced a stream of air through the lips and into the trumpet. The reed systems in the instrument were so fashioned that they produced such simple French words as *oui* and *non,* or "yes" and "no."

One Canadian inventor late in the nineteenth century constructed a metal-and-wood automaton known as The Steam Man. Inside the chest of this life-sized figure was a cone-shaped boiler that burned coal. Surrounding the boiler and filling the rest of the chest cavity was water. When the boiler was fired up, it soon heated the water and steam was produced. The steam was piped down the automaton's back and into its groin area, where it operated a piston in a cylinder. As the cutaway diagram shows, the back-and-forth action of the piston turned a flywheel, which was connected to a rod-and-shaft linkage system in the automaton's legs so as to create up and down motions. The motions were timed so that they operated a knee joint and a foot movement at the ankle. When in operation, the automaton's mechanical legs moved like those of a human being and propelled the figure forward. The exhaust steam from the cylinder was piped up to the automaton's mouth where, once every cycle the steam engine completed, it blew a whistle.

Cross-section view of The Steam Man, a metal and wood automaton constructed by a Canadian inventor in the late nineteenth century.

The Steam Man had his limitations, however. Since he was attached to a horizontal radius arm, he could only walk in circles. Moreover, he was reported to be unbearably noisy and once in a while his boiler became overheated and blew out, sending scalding water and clouds of steam in all directions.

Among the last examples of performing automatons in the tradition of Maillardet and Jacquet-

Performing automatons created by the inventor J. N. Maskelyne, as displayed in the 1876 World's Fair in Paris. To the left of the three musicians squats Psycho who performed card tricks. On the right is Zoë who drew pictures.

Droz were those created by the London inventor, J. N. Maskelyne. Displayed to large and admiring audiences, they were one of the main attractions at the 1876 World's Fair in Paris. At the center of Maskelyne's exhibit were three mustachioed musicians who played tunes on various brass instruments. To one side of them sat Zoë, a young Victorian lass who drew pictures. On the other side squatted Psycho, clad in turban and gypsy attire. The star of the show, Psycho, amazed his onlookers with feats of card playing. All five figures operated with much the same spring-driven mechanisms as the Maillardet Automaton at the Franklin Institute.

With the coming of the twentieth century and the mechanized age it brought, the days of the marvelous automatons were numbered. These mechanisms had grown so complicated that, as their ingenious inventors died out, nobody remained with the necessary skills and craftsmanship to construct them. What supplanted the automatons were clockwork toys and dolls that were produced on a mass scale.

Yet the automatons were harbingers of the robots of today. The spring-driven clockwork that

activated them has been replaced by electromechanical power, but the mechanical principles by
which the automatons moved, played instruments, wrote, and otherwise entertained audiences are the same ones that govern the intricate
movements performed by modern robots. In developing early manipulator arms for industrial
robots, engineers and designers closely studied
the elaborate linkages so meticulously worked out
by such master automatonists as Maillardet and
Jacquet-Droz. As this century progressed and
more and more machines capable of doing human
work were developed, robotics engineers ex-
panded on these principles. For example, a modern transfer robot positioning a part in a trimming
press works by much the same mechanical laws
as does the arm of the Maillardet Automaton
when it moves and writes.

As the classic automatons were making their
appearance, inventors were experimenting with
another principle that would be fundamental to
modern robotics. This was the principle of *feedback*, which makes possible the intelligence control systems or "brains" of robots in the form of
electronic computers. In essence, feedback con-

sists of trial and error and then a self-correction. Your body operates on the feedback principle: when you reach for something, small signals are transmitted from eye to brain to arm and back again. Have your arms moved far enough toward the object? Are your fingers opened wide enough to grasp it? Your brain corrects and then approves these movements and the object is successfully retrieved.

While human beings have always used feedback in this way, they did not learn to apply it to machines until many centuries had passed. When they did, the application was in regulating devices that incorporated the feedback principle of automatic self-correction. Two early examples of the feedback idea in machines occurred in the eighteenth century, both in England.

In 1745, Edmund Lee made his living by using his windmill to saw wood into lumber. Yet he often had difficulty in pointing the heavy windmill directly into the wind. Finally he hit on the idea of mounting two smaller windmills behind and at 90 degree angles to the blades of the main windmill. As long as the main windmill faced in the right wind direction, the blades of the small windmills

The feedback windmill invented by Edmund Lee in England in 1745.

did not rotate. But when the wind shifted, the smaller blades of one or the other of the small mills caught some wind and began to spin. When they did so, they turned a set of gears joined to the central axle, which in turn faced the big windmill directly into the wind again. Here was a true feedback situation: When an undesirable condition developed (the shifting of the wind), it generated a correcting force that automatically righted the situation (faced the main blades the right way).

While the self-correcting windmill never became a mechanism of great importance to civilization, the feedback principle it employed made other machines far more efficient. In the 1770s,

James Watt used feedback in regulating the speed of his steam engines. Watt wanted to control his engine so that, even with fluctuations in steam pressure, it would run at one steady velocity all the time. So he devised the flyball governor, a simple system of flyballs, or weights, spinning on a vertical shaft driven by the engine. The weights were mounted on the shaft on lever arms so that, as the shaft turned, the flyballs, driven by centrifugal force, tended to fly outward. The flyballs were also mechanically linked to a lever that opened and closed the throttle of the engine. If the engine was running too fast, the balls would fly outward due to increased centrifugal force, causing the lever to close the throttle and let less steam into the engine. With less steam the engine's speed dropped and, due to reduced centrifugal force, the balls lowered on their arms. When the engine's speed had dropped far enough, the governor would cause the throttle to open again and let more steam in. This operation was thus entirely automatic and self-regulating. Once the governor was set to the desired speed range, it required no attention.

These early examples of machines that controlled themselves by feedback were followed by other milestones in the evolution of computer technology—the technology so essential to robotics. In 1801, a French weaver named Joseph Jacquard modified a loom so that it could automatically make cloth with complicated patterns woven into the material. The loom was quite a complex device but basically it worked this way: A succession of pasteboard cards with holes punched in them was pressed against the bank of needles. These needles controlled the warp threads, the lengthwise-running threads on the loom. One

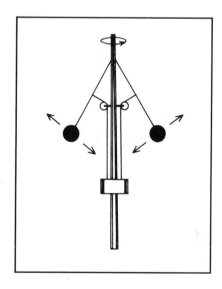

The flyball governor invented by James Watt.

card was used for each pass of the shuttle, the instrument that passed the woof thread between the crossing warp threads. The solid parts of the card pushed certain needles back out of the way of the shuttle of the loom, but holes in the card allowed other needles to remain upward and in place. These latter needles were connected to certain warp threads. When the lifting frame raised them, they raised the warp threads as well. The shuttle then made its pass with the woof thread. Then another punched card was used to leave a different set of elevated needles for the next pass, and so on until the design was woven into the material. The cards merely saved Jacquard the trouble of depressing the unwanted needles by hand on each pass of the shuttle. Jacquard's system controlled as many as 1200 needles at once.

In essence, what Jacquard did with his punched cards was to establish a language for communicating with the loom. It was confined to just two words: *hole* and *no hole*. Thus this French weaver foreshadowed the same *binary* system that is all but universal in communicating with machines today. In a binary system there are always two possible choices. The binary language of a light bulb, for instance, is simply *on* and *off*. However, these two responses can be made to symbolize whatever people wish them to: *go / don't go; no / yes; 0 / 1*. Using a number of lights, a whole vocabulary can be developed, with various combinations of *on*'s and *off*'s made to represent the letters of the alphabet. Modern machines use electric signals rather than lights. The presence or absence of signals constitutes a simple binary language into which information or instructions in any form—for example, a command to a robot to position a part in a certain way for welding—can be "translated" and fed into the machine.

Inspired by the work of Jacquard, a mathematics professor named Charles Babbage was the first man to think of feeding punched card information into a machine rather than a loom. For forty years he labored trying to build an "analytical engine," which today is considered to be the theoretical forerunner of the electronic computer. Babbage envisioned a complex calculating machine that would carry any mathematical instructions fed into it by a punched-card system. However, the Babbage engine failed in the end because of a limited metalworking industry that was incapable of engineering the parts its inventor required. Babbage died in 1871, surrounded by gear wheels, drawings, and other fragments of his unfulfilled dream.

This dream was realized by a brilliant statistician named Herman Hollerith who, in order to tabulate the United States Census of 1890, succeeded in working out a punched-card system to do the job. The holes on each card—one for each person counted—were arranged in a code pattern that stood for all the information the census takers gathered, such as the person's age, city of residence, number of children, and so forth. When tabulated, each card was slid over a number of tiny cups filled with mercury. Then rows of carefully adjusted pins were brought down on the card. Wherever they met a hole, they passed through it to the mercury beneath, completing electrical circuits that registered the results on counting dials. Pins blocked by the solid surface of the cards registered nothing. Hollerith's ingenious punched-card system allowed the census takers to complete their task in a third of the time required for the Census of 1880.

Since Hollerith's time, ways of communicating

with machines—especially in robotics—have been greatly refined. Specially trained people called programers translate instructions into symbolic language that is then electronically spelled out in the binary vocabulary inside the machine. The circuitry of the machine shunts the electric pulses through to their destinations at a speed as high as a million or more in a second, much as boxcars are switched from track to track in a crowded freightyard. In the paths of the pulses are switches which, depending on whether they are open or closed, either permit the pulses through or deflect them, according to programed instructions. And the pulses always speak the two-word machine language—*on* or *off; stop* or *go; open* or *close; yes* or *no.*

Instructions are fed into today's machines in three main ways: by punched card, by punched tape of paper or plastic, or by magnetic tape. With punched cards or tape, the instructions to be given are conveyed by means of the holes punched in meaningful combinations. The machine receives the messages of the holes through built-in "reading" devices—sensors or detectors—which sense the presence of the holes, con-

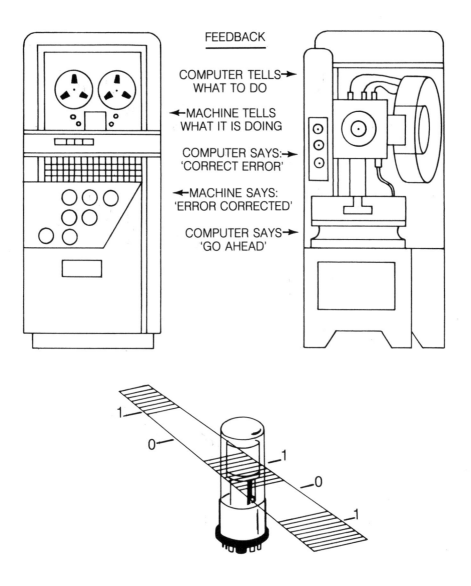

FEEDBACK

COMPUTER TELLS→
WHAT TO DO

←MACHINE TELLS
WHAT IT IS DOING

COMPUTER SAYS:→
'CORRECT ERROR'

←MACHINE SAYS:
'ERROR CORRECTED'

COMPUTER SAYS→
'GO AHEAD'

1

0

1

0

1

An electronic switch in modern computers and calculators uses the binary system. It registers "1" when conducting current and "0" when there is no pulse.

vert them into electric pulses, and flash them on into the circuitry. Most modern industrial robots use the magnetic tape method of giving instructions. The tape carries a number of channels on it, each of which is divided into spots, or "bits," which correspond to the punched holes on cards or paper tape. Sometimes there are as many as 1000 bits per inch of tape. Instructions are placed on the tape by magnetizing the bits with an electromagnetic programing control. When the tape is fed into the robot, the magnetized bits travel past a reading device, or sensor, that converts them into the binary language of electric pulses—often at speeds of over half a million bits a second.

In the 1940s, technological events were paving the way for the first successful electronic computers—truly the heart and soul of modern robots. There are two basic kinds of computers: *analog,* from the Greek *analogos,* meaning "ratio" or "proportion"; and *digital,* from the Latin *digitus,* or "finger," so named for the practice of computing with our fingers. Analog computers deal not in numbers but measurable quantities such as electric voltages, resistances, rotations, and so on; the answers they come up with are likewise expressed in physical terms. The speedometer on a car is a simple analog computer, converting a shaft's rate of rotation into mile-an-hour terms.

Digital computers, on the other hand, literally calculate and compute; their basic output is numbers. An adding machine is a digital computer because it adds one and one and one—that is, it deals in digits. The human brain is also a kind of digital computer. It is an aggregation of neurons, or nerve cells, tiny switches that are either on or off like a computer's switches. The electronic digital computer—the electronic "brain"—became the "thinking" component of modern robots.

Because a digital computer is composed of switches that have just two positions—on or off—it is by necessity committed to a binary language, a language based on two. Our decimal system uses ten numbers; digital computers use only two—values generally represented by the digits 1 and 0. These numbers correspond to the on and off positions of the switches in the computer's circuitry. Digital computers "live" on electric pulses—literally millions of them every second—which are coded in the binary system—the numbers 1 and 0—and fed into the machine via punched cards, punched tape, or magnetic tape.

The earliest digital computing machines used simple switches, but later models employed electromechanical switches called *relays* in their circuitry. These were electrically operated switches that allowed one circuit to pass on, or relay, control over other circuits. Hence, more circuits could be used to handle more impulses, and faster calculations could be made. However, these circuits could not have operated effectively without vacuum tubes, which had been invented by Dr. Lee De Forest years before. Electric impulses cannot be relayed on forever without growing weak; they must be boosted, or amplified, and this is what the somewhat bulky vacuum tubes did in early computers. In time, vacuum tubes were replaced by the tinier, far more effective transistors, and other advanced devices were built into circuits as well. One was a "flip-flop" switch. An electric pulse of current sets the flip-flop in one position and the next flips it to its other position.

The prime milestone in computer technology was ENIAC (*Electronic Numerical Integrator And Calculator*),the world's first all-electronic dig-

This early UNIVAC computer was of great proportions compared to modern miniaturized computers.

ital computer, which went into operation in 1946 at the University of Pennsylvania. An enormous device, it sprawled over 1400 square feet, weighed over thirty tons, and contained 18,000 vacuum tubes and 1500 relays. Despite its size, ENIAC had a thinking capacity equal to only a few thousand nerve cells—biologically the equivalent of the brain of a small worm. Nevertheless, it was able, in thirty seconds, to do the work that took an ordinary calculator of the day twenty hours to do. A little later ENIAC was followed by BINAC and UNIVAC which, although faster and smaller, were still of great size.

Today the dimensions of digital computers, including those used in robotics, have shrunk drastically. Many are so small they can be held in one's hand. Old-fashioned wiring—miles of it in early computers—has given way to small printed-circuit panels. And the transistor, which replaced the venerable vacuum tube, has become miniaturized and even subminiaturized. These ultra-tiny transistors are now being built into integrated-circuit silicon wafers, or "chips," which further reduce the size of components in computers. It is now possible to place more than 500,000 step-by-step logic circuits on a single wafer.

Another robotics milestone was the gradual development of the mechanical hand-and-arm in the late 1950s. Early attempts at making these employed some of the linkage systems of the nineteenth-century automatonists. The arms were really crude grasping devices, operated manually as extensions of human hands, for pouring and otherwise manipulating dangerous chemicals in laboratories. The operator pushed and pulled lever handles or twisted dial wheels that were mechanically linked to shafts that could rotate in either direction. The shafts, in turn, were geared to open or close the grasping "fingers" so that the hand could clutch, say, a beaker and manipulate it. By another linkage system, the operator could control a mechanically jointed "elbow" whereby the grasping device was moved backward or forward or left or right as needed. In time, electric motor power was wedded to these mechanisms to make the operator's task easier.

One of the biggest breakthroughs in hand-and-arm technology came when engineers hit on the idea of a sliding tube within a tube—using the principle of a piston and cylinder—that greatly simplified the manipulating action of robot arms. This development also eliminated many of the complicated old automatonist linkage arrangements. In its several varieties, it is employed in many industrial robots today.

Basically, such a manipulator arm consists of a main tube and within it a close-fitting, well-oiled smaller tube that can slide in and out; it can rotate as well. The sliding action can be accomplished by a number of mechanical means. One early method employed a pulley-wheel system such as the ones seen on dentists' drills. The system on the dentist's drill causes a bit or burr to rotate at high speed, but the system on the manipulator

A Unimate robot at work in a factory. The sliding tubes within tubes to extend or contract the reach of the robot's arm can clearly be seen.

arm made the smaller tube slide back and forth in the bigger tube—extending or reducing the "reach" of the robot.

This basic tube-within-a-tube arm of modern robots is mounted on a base or trunk that is also capable of movement. Because it is built to swivel, the base can rotate the arm left or right in wide horizontal arcs, or sweeps. Moreover, the arm is so attached to the base that it can swing up or down vertically. All of these manipulative features give the robot arm a high degree of flexible action to perform its task. The flexibility is increased even further when a mechanical bending wrist and gripper-hand are attached to the end of the arm. Not only can the arm extend in and out, rotate left and right, and swing up and down, but the wrist-and-hand elements can be made to bend, twist, and grasp.

Mechanical bending wrist and gripper-hand of this Prab industrial robot are apparent in the photo. This model has five axes of motion; typical uses include transferring parts, tool loading and unloading, die casting, and forging.

51

ROBOTICS

Another important development was the servo-motor, or "servo." Without it modern robots simply could not operate. Servomotors are small but very powerful electric motors that can supply power for the drive train gearing that is built into a robot's arm and wrist elements. This servo-driven gearwork is what actually causes the arm to move in and out and the wrist to be manipulated into correct positions. Servos contain sensing elements that can pick up the comparatively weak binary code instruction signals from the computer control unit, amplify them, and then use the signals to actuate the servomotor. The sensing element can be a photoelectric cell or some other device that responds to the computer's coded signals. The sensing element is also an error-determining device that, using feedback, constantly compares the requirements of the computer's commands with the gear action delivered by the servo. If, say, the current decreases for a moment, that error signal itself is fed back to the amplifier to tell it to deliver the correct amount of current to the servo.

With improved manipulator arms and new advances in computer technology, control engineers in the 1950s made their first attempts to couple computer "brains" to the mechanical parts of machines. Dr. Heinrich Ernst of the Massachusetts Institute of Technology established a robotics milestone when he wedded a special electronic computer to an early sliding-tube manipulator arm. Ernst programed the robot to explore the area within reach of its gripper hand. Specifically, the machine was commanded to stack children's

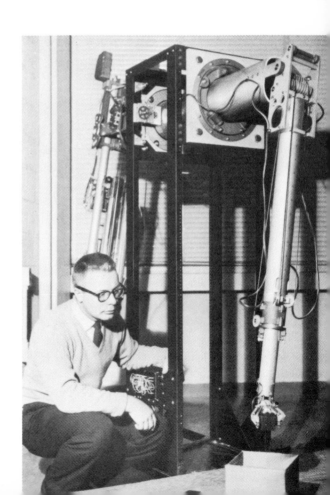

Early experimental robot arm with gripper hand at Massachusetts Institute of Technology, wedded to a computer, could stack and store children's blocks.

blocks, one on top of the other, which it did with great success.

Today's robots can be programed to do more than merely stack blocks. With their sophisticated memory systems and intricate logic circuits, they can make split-second decisions from their computer control units and order their manipulator arms, wrists, and grippers to carry them out.

So the robot, far from being an innovation of the twentieth century, had its origins in myths and its early models in ancient societies. It slowly assumed reality in toys, dolls, and the automatons created by such men as Maillardet. Along the way, science-fiction literature and film glorified the mechanical man of metal. Imaginative working models of them were built and exhibited. For instance, Westinghouse's giant aluminum robot nicknamed Elektro was a big attraction at the New York World's Fair of 1939 and later "acted" in a movie. In more recent decades, the robot even became a surrogate for human workers. And with modern electronic and mechanical technology, it has at last evolved into a reliable servant of the people.

Elektro, Westinghouse's giant aluminum robot, was a big hit
at the New York World's Fair in 1939–40. Here Elektro is
shown in a scene from the film *The Day the Earth Stood Still*.
Actress Patricia Neal looks on as the robot revives his master,
actor Bruce Bennett, inside a flying saucer.

THREE

Robots in Industry

In order to understand how robots work, it is first necessary to consider what they are designed to do. Whether robots take the form of artificial humans or inhuman-looking machinery, they are constructed for one purpose: to perform the work of men and women and to do it as automatically and efficiently as possible.

Pretend for a moment that you are faced with the job of building a robot to do a specific job; for example, shoveling your driveway after every snowfall. What basic systems would you need that correspond to a human snow-shoveler? First, you would need some kind of power system. Just as people require food and drink to energize their bodies, a robot requires some kind of power to make it move and act. Second, you would have to provide your robot with a system of controllable appendages—legs and arms—that would allow it to walk along the driveway and manipulate the shovel as and where it is needed. Third, your robot would have to have an intelligence control system—a "brain"—to instruct its legs where to take it and its arms what to do. Any robot needs these three systems to function: power, working appendages, and a control system.

Whereas the energy that ran the old automatons was supplied by spring-driven clockwork or steam, modern robots are powered exclusively by electricity. As delivered by the generators of today's electrical utilities, electric power is readily available to robots almost anywhere, is comparatively cheap, and, except for occasional breakdowns at the generating plant, is steady and continuous.

The appendages of modern robots, especially

those of the industrial type, consist of some form of manipulator arm. At the end of the arm is the robot's wrist, which can swivel and so is able to hold and orient a tool of some kind, such as a welding torch, or operate a gripper-hand if the job calls for clutching. Most industrial robots are equipped with some variation of the sliding tube-within-a-tube arm. While some robots' arms still slide in and out with pulley systems, most now employ hydraulic mechanisms operated electrically. The hydraulic mechanism uses water or some other fluid under pressure to transmit the power necessary to slide the arm.

Robotic engineers have a language all their own in discussing the movements of robots' appendages. A robot's arm doesn't just "move." It "articulates," "traverses," or has a "degree of freedom" or "axis of motion." Three articulations are provided for the arm: move left or right, up or down, in or out. The maximum number of degrees the arm can swing from right to left and vice versa is known as "rotational traverse"; typical ranges are 280°, 200°, and 125°. The range over which an arm is able to move up and down is known as "vertical traverse" and is usually about 30°. Addi-

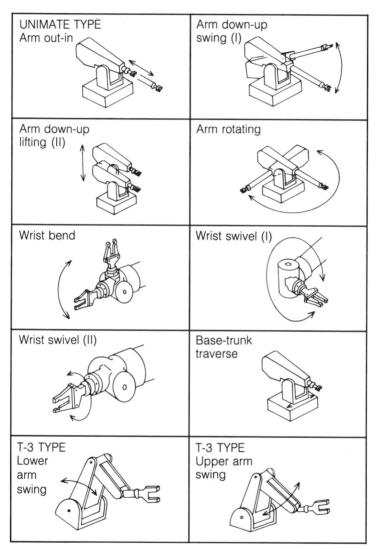

Various degrees of freedom of an industrial robot's arm.

tional degrees of freedom are built into the robot's wrist and are variously spoken of as "bend," "twist," "yaw," and "swivel."

The intelligence control system in today's robots is of course the electronic digital computer. Now that this amazing device has been so miniaturized that its circuitry can be printed or etched onto tiny silicone chips it is often called a "microprocessor." The computer—or, as robotics engineers refer to it, the control unit—is usually located on the robot's base-housing or in a separate console. It is connected to the robot's mechanical parts so that it can issue commands to them electronically. There is continual back-and-forth feedback between the programed computer and the machine's arm and wrist to maintain the desired performance on a particular job. This split-second feedback via electric pulses coded in the binary system generates what control engineers call the "error signal"—in effect, answering the robot's question of, say, "Is my wrist twisting correctly?" If the twisting motion is correct according to the computer's program, the computer flashes back the answer, "Yes." This motion is allowed to go on for perhaps five millionths of a second when, say, a yaw is required. "Wrist-yaw three degrees left," orders the computer. And so on through the task to be accomplished.

The commonest of all industrial robots is the "playback" robot, so-called because it is capable of memorizing and repeating, or playing back, a program of movements taught to it by a human operator. Suppose a playback robot is programed for a spot-welding job. The robot is set up beside a moving assembly line, which pauses before the robot for a short length of time before continuing on. In this brief interval, the robot's job is to make three spot welds on the top of a flat metal housing—one on the side nearest the robot and the other two at the far end. With the welding torch clasped in its gripper-hand, the robot will first bend its wrist down and make the spot weld on the housing's near side. But to make the second weld on the far left of the housing, the robot must extend its arm for that length and also make a rotational traverse to the left to reach the proper spot with the torch. To make the weld on the far right, the robot must make a right rotational traverse and extend its arm again slightly. After each weld, the wrist must bend upward so that the

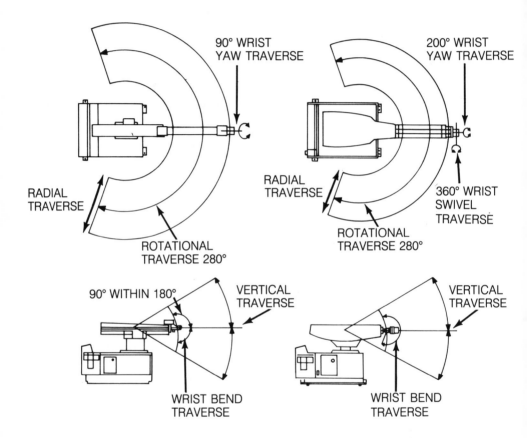

Plans and elevations of typical industrial playback robots showing such degrees of freedom as rotational and vertical traverses, minimum and maximum arm and wrist extension, and
wrist bend traverse.

torch will not weld the wrong places on the housing. In addition, this particular job calls for a wrist-swivel motion over the weld—180° clockwise and 180° counterclockwise—so that the flame is evenly applied.

In all, this welding operation may consist of a continuous sequence of thirty strategic places, called "points," in the robot's program where the machine must be commanded to do something different—for example, a wrist bend down, a clockwise swivel, an arm-out extension, a wrist bend up. These positions must be taught to the robot by an operator who moves its arm and wrist manually through the welding job, just as if he were teaching a child to write by holding a pencil in its hand and moving it across the paper. Once this sequence of steps is programed into the robot's control unit, the robot can repeat them accurately.

A program point, however, consists of more than orienting the robot's arm and wrist to certain positions in space. It consists also of functional and speed data. For example, certain points in the welding operation may call for a DELAY function, when the robot's motion ceases for a split second before resuming. Or a point may specify a CON-TINUE function, which means the robot's motion is not stopped but continues on to the next point in the program. And the speed at which each taught point is approached must also go into the program so that the entire welding operation can be timed as the job requires.

To teach the robot, the operator uses a hand-held "teach pendant," containing push buttons, which is connected to the minicomputer and to a cathode ray tube display screen. When the operator, called a "setup man,"is satisfied that the arm and wrist position, function, and speed are the correct ones for a particular point, he presses the program button and this data is stored in the computer. The pendant also contains buttons that allow the operator to replay the taught program on the screen and debug it if necessary by adding or deleting points at will. If this particular welding program is to be reused later, it can be recorded on cassette tape and replayed into the robot's memory.

With the teaching process completed and the programed instructions stored in the computer, the operator can switch the robot to automatic op-

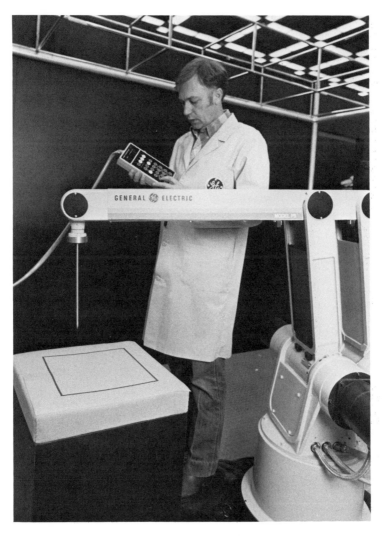

An engineer using a teach pendant to program an industrial robot.

eration and the welding job can begin. The program playback will then cause the robot to go through the taught sequence of thirty points smoothly. With the robot at the START or HOME position, the assembly line with one of the housings to be welded pauses before it. As programed, the arm and wrist go through their first sequence of thirty points and complete the weld on the near side of the housing.

Now consider what happens on some typical points of the second weld. With the arm having extended to position the wrist and gripper directly over the spot to be welded, the computer instructs the robot to execute point fourteen, which consists of a wrist-down movement to bring the torch into contact with the metal housing. As the point fourteen signals are received by the wrist servo's sensor, they are amplified many times until they are boosted to the necessary electrical wattage to activate the servomotor. All the while the sensor is checking back and forth hundreds of times a second with the computer and amplifier to self-correct any error that may occur. These boosted signals also contain the orientation position to which the servo's gears will bend the wrist and gripper—in this case, straight down to make the weld contact.

When feedback circuits inform the computer that point fourteen has been successfully completed, the playback program tape moves to point fifteen and sends out coded instructions for it. As before, these are received by the servo sensor, boosted by the amplifier, and fed to the geared servomotor of the wrist. However, this time the gears do not move for several thousandths of a second, because point fifteen contains the programed function WAIT for that length of time to allow the torch to heat and fuse the weld. Next in sequence, points sixteen and seventeen call for the clockwise and counterclockwise rotary wrist swivels of 180° to apply the torch's flame evenly over the spot weld area. With the second weld completed, point eighteen contains instructions to bend the wrist and gripper up, away from the housing.

To move on to the third and final weld, the robot now needs new reach and traverse commands. Point nineteen supplies the first of these by issuing instructions to a servo in the robot's swivel base to make a rotational traverse of so many degrees to the right. This traverse sweeps the arm around so that it is pointing directly toward the third weld area. But the wrist is still a few inches short of it. Programed point twenty remedies this situation with signals to the servo built into the robot's arm, and its reach is extended so that the wrist is oriented directly over the last weld area. The robot then goes through the rest of the points in its taught cycle, completing the last weld and returning to its START or HOME position on the thirtieth point. The assembly line, synchronized with the time it takes the robot to do its work, now moves the welded housing along and moves the next one into position to be welded. As programed, the robot then repeats the same sequence of thirty taught points to weld the next housing.

On more complicated jobs, of course, the number of taught points in a program would be greater. Many larger playback robots are capable of learning several hundred point-sequences and some can perform as many as 1500. Playback robots can also be set up and programed to "branch" from one point-sequence to another and to switch to other tools held by the gripper-hand. While the spot-welding example assumed an assembly line that stopped momentarily in front of the robot, most larger playback robots can be set up to track and execute a taught-point sequence on a continuously moving assembly line. In addition, newer and faster teaching methods are being developed to cut down on valuable setup time. One, numerical control, allows the operator to feed numerical point-coordinates to the computerized control unit instead of setting them by hand.

Because of the high cost of modern sophisticated playback robots, machines called "sequence robots" are also in wide use today. Sequence robots cost less because the manufacturer builds the program directly into the machine's hardware. Although the manufacturer can adjust the sequence robot to do a number of different jobs, it is extremely difficult for the user to change the program or add new ones. The robot only moves along a straight line from point to point and is suitable for such simple jobs as transferring materials from one station on a production line to another. The great advantage of sequence robots is their price: they cost anywhere from $5000 to $32,000, compared to $45,000 to $70,000 for playback robots. The sequence robot is a useful alternative for users who want to automate their operations but who do not need the complexity and dexterity of a playback robot.

Two early experimenters whose patented research led to the creation of the playback robot were George Duvol and Thomas James. A brilliant engineer named Joseph F. Engelberger built on their pioneer work and has succeeded better than anyone else in introducing working robots into industry. Beginning in the late 1950s with industrial models, he was by 1961 actually testing one

A typical layout of an assembly line combining Puma robots and manual work stations.

on an assembly line at General Motors Corporation.

Engelberger named his robots Unimates, and they are at work today in the factories of most major industrial nations. Already they have logged over ten million man-hours of industrial tasks of various kinds. Unimates and other industrial robots are manufactured by Unimation, Inc., the world's largest manufacturer of industrial robots, and Joseph Engelberger is one of its chief officers.

Modern Unimate playback robots are widely used to weld cars and trucks for many of the world's major auto manufacturers. On one assembly line some 230 feet long at General Motors, twenty Unimates toil in tandem, putting components into the correct position on a car's underbody, then welding them into place. As the frames are fed from one Unimate team to another, one robot positions the part, while its partner does the welding. Because the Unimates must work on the moving assembly line, the appropriate instructions to do so have been included in their taught-points programs. At the end of the line, an inspection robot checks to see if the welding and positioning has been done correctly. Robot production lines of this same type are in use in Sweden, Japan, and Germany.

Playback robots can be set up and taught point-sequence programs for just about any industrial job imaginable. They can handle large and unwieldy parts at the rate of 400 pieces per hour with no change in their cycle time and are adaptable for long- or short-run operations. They can feed forging presses and produce molds for metal castings. They can flame, rout, polish, and grind. They can paint with a spray gun, ladle molten metal, operate trimming presses, perform lubrication jobs, cast dies, and perform many other operations. When products or processes change, the robot's gripper can readily be adjusted to accommodate whatever new tool is necessary.

Since the playback speeds on these robots are independent of the actual teaching speeds, point-sequence programs taught slowly by the operator can be speeded up and still be performed accurately. More detailed point-sequences can also be taught for very complex operations where, say, the robot's wrist must momentarily shift the gripper to other equipment. Moreover, playback machines like Unimate can be programed to teach

A team of Unimate industrial robot welders working in tandem on an automobile production line.

other Unimates the point-sequences it has learned—even to sister Unimates in another plant. Hence, it is only necessary to teach one Unimate a learned-points program to set a whole team of them to work on a particular operation. While most playback robots perform from a stationary base, some are designed to work on a traverse base, which moves, to increase their freedom.

Another kind of playback robot in wide use today employs an arm-manipulation system different from the Unimate type. Instead of having the single sliding tube arrangement whereby the arm goes in and out, this robot uses a jointed-arm configuration that gives it six rotary axes of movement. As can be seen in the diagram, these axes consist of arm sweep, shoulder swivel, and elbow extension, as well as the pitch, yaw, and roll orientations of the wrist. The elbow axis is driven by a piston-cylinder arrangement that is servomotor-controlled by the machine's minicomputer. Like the sliding tube playback robots, the jointed-arm robots are taught their designated tasks on a point-sequence basis by a setup man with a teach pendant. While a number of the jointed-arm models are manufactured, one of the most popular among users is The Tomorrow Tool, or T3, made by Cincinnati Milachron, second largest producer of industrial robots in the United States. The T3 is used by many firms to weld base assemblies for computer frames, position parts, load and unload, inspect castings, and to perform jobs in close quarters where great flexibility is needed.

A multiple exposure photograph of a T3 industrial robot showing its many degrees of freedom.

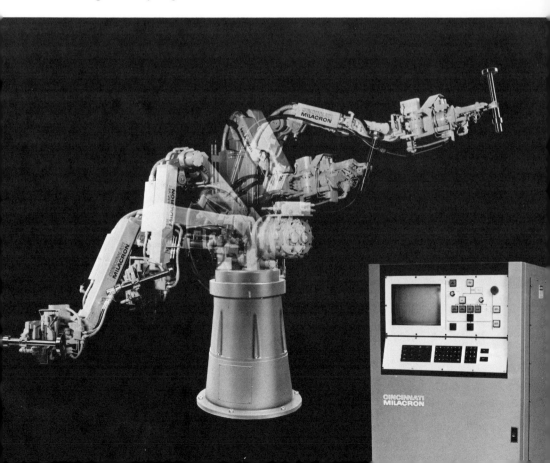

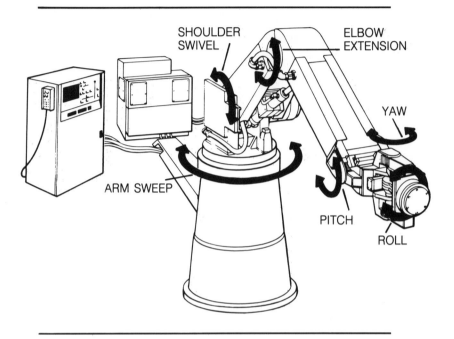

SHOULDER
SWIVEL

ELBOW
EXTENSION

YAW

ARM SWEEP

PITCH

ROLL

Nomenclature and unit elements of a T3 industrial robot.

Because the sequence robots are far lower in cost than the programable playback robots, far more of them are in use today around the world than the expensive playbacks, especially by smaller manufacturers, who often rent rather than buy them. They are frequently used for simply transferring parts or materials from one station to another, and so they are sometimes called "transfer robots." More often than not sequence robots use some form of the sliding tube arm with wrist for manipulation. In addition to their transfer capabilities, these machines are ideal for such repetitive jobs as stamping out parts, oiling, cutting, gluing, sorting, capping bottles, and positioning and assembling components. One Japanese watchmaking company, Seiko, has totally automated its assembly operation by using sequence minirobots.

A special kind of industrial robot named Mobot

A display of Seiko sequence minirobots designed for automatic small watch part feeding and transfer systems. The Japanese firm began developing these robots over thirty years ago for more efficient assembling of their watches.

can manipulate dangerous materials like toxic chemicals at a distance. The name, coined by the Hughes Aircraft Company, which first developed it, comes from *m*anipulated *robot*. First used in atomic research centers, early Mobots were fixed to one spot, able only to do work within reach of their arms guided awkwardly by operators behind thick leaded-glass windows. Later models were mounted on wheels so that they could be steered around to perform their tasks. Gradually they acquired television eyes, microphone ears, and other sensing organs to monitor temperature and radiation levels. Operated by human beings seated at remote control panels away from the danger area, earlier Mobots were controlled by electrical wiring that carried the commands to activate arm and gripper motors.

In today's Mobots, the electrical wiring has been replaced by radio command-guidance control. Their arms are often of the double-jointed type for greater flexibility, although sometimes a sliding tube arrangement is used in the outer limb to extend the wrist and gripper for slight distances. As in the industrial playback robots, servos are built into the jointed arm and wrist; when activated by command, they do the manipulating. There the similarity ends, however. Mobots are not controlled by programed computers but by human operators monitoring their movements via closed-circuit TV remote from the danger area. Seated at his console, the operator transmits radio-signal commands to the shoulder, arm, or wrist servos. These are picked up, amplified, and fed into the motor which, when activated, moves the appropriate limb a certain distance.

In a typical operation, say pouring a corrosive chemical liquid from one flask to another, the operator would use a Mobot Mark II, which has two arms. From his console he sends radio signals to the servo in the joint of the first arm to sweep close to the laboratory table where the two flasks have been placed. More radio commands to the wrist servo instruct it to open its padded gripper fingers to accommodate the neck of the flask with the liquid in it. Then, in tiny increments of rotary sweep movements, he instructs the shoulder servo to advance the wrist and gripper until its fingers are on either side of the neck. The next radio commands instruct the padded fingers to close slowly until the flask is firmly grasped. The opera-

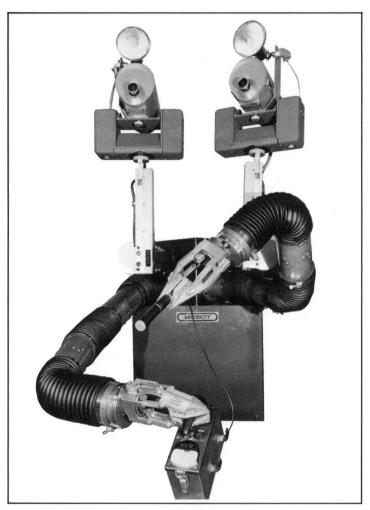

Display photograph of a Mobot Mark II robot operating a Geiger counter. Actually, the counter is usually built into the robot so that the robot's versatile hands are free for maneuvering.

tor then orders a vertical upswing at the shoulder joint of a few degrees and the flask is picked up. Another rotary traverse of the arm sweeps the wrist out to the front of the robot where the pouring will take place.

Similar radio commands from the operator cause the second arm to pick up the empty flask and position it correctly to receive the pour. Radio signals are now sent for a slow rotary twist downward of the first arm's wrist. The gripper fingers delicately upend the flask holding the liquid and the pour is completed. A skilled Mobot operator will seldom spill a drop. Such Mobots are often equipped with a set of tank treads on which the machine can be moved from one job to another. Mobots are often equipped with built-in Geiger counters to test radiation levels in areas that may be dangerous to humans.

Oftentimes modern industrial robots are sensor-aided to help them perform their tasks more efficiently. The sensor, frequently a photocell, may be in the wrist portion of the robot itself or it can be located apart from the robot but near the particular workpiece it is concerned with. The sensor can, for example, sense that a tool held in the gripper is wrongly positioned. The sensor can then signal the computer by feedback to stop the point-sequence cycle until the error is corrected.

A sensor-aided robot is nearly always used as the inspection robot at the end of an assembly line. One of these, built by the Auto-Place Corporation, employs a laser beam sensor to check and approve the critical shapes and sizes of machine parts. While the robot holds the part in its gripper, the beam is guided by an intricate system of mirrors through and around the part, checking its exact dimensions. This information is fed back to the computer, which then makes the decision whether or not the part is within acceptable tolerances.

With industrial robotics booming, one might well wonder how many robots are in operation in plants and factories around the world today. In 1982 the Robot Industry Association announced figures for a survey of the number of programable robots (excluding the fixed-program sequence robots) then in use. In round figures, there were approximately 4000 such robots in the United States; 2300 in West Germany; 1000 in France; 600 in Sweden; and 500 in Great Britain. No fig-

A sensor-aided Opto-Sense robot made by Auto-Place Corporation. Its laser mode provides speed-of-light recognition for "yes/no" decision-making and sorting. The system is based on a receptor or interruption of a laser beam to make its decisions.

ures were given for the Soviet Union, China, or other nations. But the world's leading user of industrial robots is not the United States. It is Japan, which has some 14,000 programable robots in operation today.

This means that at present roughly two-thirds of the world's programable robot force is at work in various industries in the Japanese home islands. Many of them, such as Unimates, were purchased in the United States, but Japanese robot-makers like Kawasaki Heavy Industries have also been turning out their own machines for several years and improving technology in the field of sensory robots. The Japanese are also big users of sequence robots in light industry. These machines have dramatically improved the country's industrial productivity and quality control and are expected to extend Japan's current trade advantage over the United States. Furthermore, they are expected to compensate for a crippling labor shortage in Japan and to rescue many small businessmen and industrialists, who can now take advantage of low rates to rent robots.

FOUR

Robots in Home and Office

We have in our homes today many mechanisms that qualify as robots because they do what robots were created to do: perform useful human work and do it automatically. A look around any typical dwelling place will reveal a dozen or so robots—dishwashers, clock-radios, refrigerators, record players, water heaters, to name only a few—without which we would find modern living difficult indeed.

The manufacturers of these household robots

have built into them either one of two basic control principles. One is known as open-loop control. Recalling the nineteenth century automatons, this kind of control makes it possible for a machine, once started, to proceed as if by clockwork through a pre-established pattern of performance. Open loop controls abound in today's homes: in the start-to-stop functioning of an automatic washing machine, a record changer, a coffee maker. But once they have completed their performance cycle, they must be reset and reactivated by human intervention. In other words, it takes a person to close the "loop" between the end of a machine's performance and the restarting of it.

The other principle, called "closed-loop control," or more familiarly, feedback, requires no human intervention to close the loop. As with Watt's governor and Edmund Lee's windmill, this type of control makes it possible for a machine to check, correct, and self-control its own operations while they are in progress. Two common household robots, one employing open loop and the other closed loop, are practically fixtures in every modern house today: the automatic toaster and the thermostat that controls the furnace. Both employ metal sensors, but with different results.

In the automatic toaster, the sequence begins when the bread is placed in the toaster and the handle is depressed. When the handle hits bottom, it is locked in place by a latch on a switch. The handle also closes the switch and completes a circuit, allowing electric current to flow to the toasting coils, which glow red-hot and cook the bread. The handle has also closed a second switch, which allows current to flow into a small heating coil beside the sensor. The sensor is a thin bar made of strips of metal that expand at different rates. The coil's heat makes the bottom strip expand faster, bending the sensor up until it hits the second switch and turns it off. With its circuit broken, the heating coil cools, and the sensor bends down again. When it hits the first switch, it turns off the toasting coils, releasing the springed handle and popping up the toast. However, to carry out the same set of mechanical sequences to make new toast, a human being is needed to depress the handle again.

By contrast, the furnace control thermostat can regulate itself by feedback without human intervention. The robot thermostat contains a heat-sensitive metal sensor of the same type used in the automatic toaster. When heated it can bend and either make or break electric circuits that switch the furnace on or off. If the thermostat is set at 68° Fahrenheit and the room temperature drops below that figure, the metal sensor bends, makes switch-contact, and kicks the furnace back on again. When the temperature has risen to the desired level, the thermostat shuts off the furnace. This relationship of furnace to room temperature to thermostat and back to furnace is direct, interacting, self-regulatory, and closed, as in a chain or loop—hence the term closed loop control. This same control principle also regulates our refrigerators and air-conditioners.

In the world of business, the number and variety of robotic devices is staggering—and becoming more so as electronic and mechanization advances are made. Despite their diversity and complexity, many of these robots still perform their tasks for us on a recognizable open or closed loop basis. Silent and efficient elevators, with no operator necessary, whisk workers to offices dozens of stories high and down again, and nearly

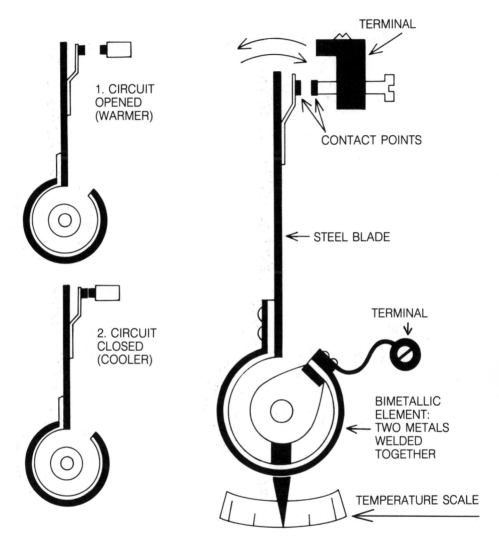

1. CIRCUIT OPENED (WARMER)

2. CIRCUIT CLOSED (COOLER)

TERMINAL

CONTACT POINTS

STEEL BLADE

TERMINAL

BIMETALLIC ELEMENT: TWO METALS WELDED TOGETHER

TEMPERATURE SCALE

A furnace-control robot thermostat can regulate itself by feed-back without human intervention.

all are equipped with automatic sliding doors. Essentially they can be considered open-loop robots, for someone somewhere must push a button to activate them. Robot sprinklers are installed in all office ceilings, set to switch on automatically in case of fire; like air-conditioners and furnace controls, they contain temperature sensitive closed-loop thermostats.

The electronic digital computer is at the heart of today's modern business operations. As the brain controlling so many robotic devices, it is an absolute necessity. Highly complex and sensitive machines, these business robots have moved into and automated such fields as banking, accounting, airlines, supermarkets, the stock market, warehousing, and government, to name only a few.

A typical example is the banking robot known as ERMA, whose initials stand for *Electronic Recording Method of Accounting*. Actually a robot paper processor, it was developed to save the banking industry from drowning in oceans of paperwork. In its original version, introduced in the 1960s, the processor covered several thousand square feet of floor space. But with the miniaturization achieved in electronics and computers since then, modern versions can fit into even small banks with ease. Acting like an assembly line, an ERMA-type processor can sort, post, record, and update thousands of bank accounts in an hour, if it has to.

By almost instantaneous feedback between its computer and memory elements and its magnetic sensor "eyes," this processor can read and digest information on accounts, make decisions, and print out hundreds of lines of banking data in a single minute. When handling checks, its writing duties include printing out the signatures of bank executives. This processor can easily handle twice as many accounts in one minute as a bank clerk can in an hour. It thus frees humans from the boredom of "making marks on paper," a task that constitutes a good portion of the banking industry.

Businesses and government agencies are also finding another kind of robot absolutely indispensable: the information storage and retrieval robot. Depending on the particular field, informa-

An ERMA-type robot bank processor can handle twice as many accounts in one minute as a human clerk can in an hour.

tion of all kinds—abstracts of articles, license plate numbers, insurance data, fingerprints, engineering specifications—can be stored in miniaturized memory drums and banks. Each individual unit of information is coded with a special magnetic marking. When that information is needed, magnetic robot sensors scan through the memory systems at split-second speed, locate it by matching up the request with the correct coding, and either print the information out or display it on a screen. The Internal Revenue Service uses such retrieval robots to search literally miles of magnetic tape to check information on income tax statements.

In the legal field especially, the automatic information retrieval systems have been of immense help. Rather than spending valuable time searching through lawbooks for precedents, a lawyer can avail himself of computerized retrieval services to locate this information for him and even help him to prepare his brief. One group of lawyers recently suggested that robot retrieval apparatus might be developed to predict Supreme Court decisions. Laws and decisions handed down previously would be recorded in an electronic memory system. The robot would then be able to screen the memory for whatever might apply to the case in question. These lawyers have also predicted that such robotized legal assistants may one day be used to streamline court proceedings so that the present backlog of cases in the courts can be cleared away—never to build up again.

Automated libraries, linked by radio or telephone to other libraries across the country, are already benefiting scholars, writers, and ordinary readers as well. Students especially are taking advantage of this exchange-of-information service to prepare assignments and term papers. If the library does not have the particular information the student wants, electronic memory checks can be made of other libraries in the system to turn up the books, magazines, or other material he or she requires.

So, as they have in industry, robots have made themselves indispensable in our homes and offices. It would be hard indeed to run our modern world without them, for the chores they perform are the services to which we have become accustomed.

FIVE

Robots in Science, Medicine and Space

Scientists have long been interested in how living creatures use their brains to make decisions and solve problems. Some early research in this area of inquiry was actually done with man-made robot "animals." One American scientist named Edmund Berkeley built a mechanical "squirrel" that rolled around on battery-powered wheels and could search out and locate objects. And an English scientist, W. Grey Walter, constructed a series of mechanical "tortoises" that also rolled about under battery power and could successfully avoid obstacles placed in their way.

Both Berkeley's and Walter's robot "animals" were fitted with photocell "eyes" to "see" their way. Photocells produce electric current when light shines on them, and that current can be made to do work, such as tripping relay switches. Each of the scientists employed a powerful lamp as the light source while their robots rolled around on the floor. The objects to be located or avoided reflected light to the robots' photocell "eyes," and these then produced current that tripped relay switches connected to the rolling wheels. In this way, the wheels could be switched to advance or retreat, depending on whether the robot was supposed to find an object or avoid it. Both Berkeley and Grey later added simple computer systems to their robots so that they could be made to learn and carry out a sequence of events.

Perhaps the best known of the robot animals was an electromechanical "mouse" constructed by Claude Shannon, a scientist working at Bell Laboratories in the early 1950s. The mouse was, in reality, a two-inch bar magnet with three wheels and copper whiskers. Shannon built a large maze with aluminum gates that could be altered to create the hardest possible problems for the mouse. Its task was to thread its way through a certain path set up by Shannon and reach "a piece of cheese," which was actually an electrical terminal with a bell that rang when the mouse nudged it with its copper whiskers. Shannon's purpose was to try to teach the robot mouse to "remember" certain problem-paths through the maze and, in so doing, to prove in a limited sense that a machine could be made to have a "memory." Shannon also hoped to learn how to improve Bell's telephone service in the process. In the mouse and its maze he used the same kind of switching relays found in dial telephone systems.

The robot mouse worked this way: When it was set down on the metal floor of the maze, it tripped an electric switch that signaled its position to a mechanism under the floor. A motor-driven electromagnet now moved swiftly to the spot directly beneath the mouse and from then on held it in its magnetic grasp. The magnet could turn through ninety-degree angles and, carrying the mouse with it, guide it forward toward the "cheese." If the mouse, in its first trial-and-error run, hit a

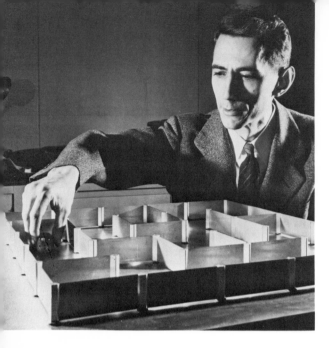

Dr. Claude Shannon of Bell Laboratories experimenting with his electrical robot mouse in 1952. Experiments with the mouse and switching relays aided researchers in thinking of new ways to use the logical powers of computers.

barrier and detected with its copper whiskers that it had come to a dead end, the magnet could back the mouse away, shift it to another direction, and start it forward again to try to find an open path. At each successful turn, a relay was correctly set and recorded in the circuitry. After scuttling up and down corridors, bumping into walls, backing up, turning, and exploring, the mouse usually took about two minutes to find the cheese and ring the bell.

Once the mouse had learned the correct path to the cheese, Dr. Shannon could program this identical path into the relay-switch system that regulated the motor-driven electromagnet underneath the maze. The mouse could then be set down at any point that it visited during its explorations and, without making a single false move, proceed directly to the goal in about twelve seconds. After altering the maze in thousands of experiments with the robot mouse, Shannon accumulated much valuable data—principally new ways of hooking up relays in circuitry—about how machines can be made to "remember." Many of these techniques have now been built into telephone dial switching, automatic accounting machines, and other equipment.

Over the years, a series of enormously complex machines known as educated robots have been constructed. Largely one-of-a-kind robots, they can do some amazing things. One called ILLIAC (*Illi*nois *A*utomatic *C*omputer) can actually compose music, including the *Illiac Suite for String Quartet*. A German robot called Zuse (Suzy) set up in a large tourist bureau can plan itineraries for travelers. A huge United States Air Force robot system known as SAGE, for *S*emi-*A*utomatic *G*round *E*nvironment, has not just one master computer control center but dozens of them to coordinate United States air defense networks. In the teaching machine field, a robot called PLATO, for *Programed Logic for Automatic Teaching Operations*, can be programed to coach, teach, and test students in several subjects—and even to reprimand the pupils with an electronic speaker system, if necessary.

Robotic science has also contributed to the field of learning. Learning involves perception: seeing and recognizing a thing or an event for what it is or represents. At Cornell University, a psychologist named Frank Rosenblatt constructed a robotic device that he called "Perceptron"—a machine that seemed to perceive and, in so doing, learn. Rosenblatt used electronic sensor nerve cells connected in a random manner in Perceptron's computer control unit. As the machine learned to do simple perceptive tasks—recognizing individual letters of the alphabet, for example—Perceptron was able to "organize" this network of cells itself, a feat no electronic "brain" had achieved before. The machine accomplished this organization by selecting circuits on a trial-and-error basis and correcting its decisions by feedback when necessary.

100

The human brain, while infinitely more complex than a machine like Perceptron, is thought to be composed of somewhat random networks of neurons or nerve cells at birth. But like Perceptron we "self-organize" those networks into learning patterns as we grow, gradually increasing our store of knowledge. Scientists are now experimenting with more sophisticated Perceptron-type robots in the hope of finding out more about how our brains function as self-organizing systems.

In marine science, Mobot prototypes and experimental models have been built for possible use underwater. When and if perfected, these Mobot divers, working with jointed arms and grippers, seeing by closed-circuit TV, and hearing with sonar apparatus, could spare human divers the dangers of undersea exploration and jobs like drilling oil wells. A few years ago, a Mobot actually went to work for the Shell Oil Company as a "roughneck" diver to drill wells on the ocean floor off California at depths of 200 feet. Costing a quarter of a million dollars, the Mobot was equipped with propellers to drive it to its underwater work site. While the Mobot performed its job well, the project eventually had to be phased out because of prohibitive costs.

In the field of medicine, one of the most exciting developments in robotics is the creation of "bionic" limbs. These prosthetic devices—artificial legs or arms—are controlled by the brain of a person equipped with one. Such a bionic arm has been developed by the Veteran's Administration. It does not enhance the strength of the wearer's arm but is designed to function as much as possible like a normal arm. Assume a wearer has lost his arm midway between the shoulder joint and the elbow. The bionic plastic arm, jointed at the elbow and wrist, is made especially to fit the wearer's upper arm stump.

At the place where the stump meets the padded surface of the bionic arm, electrical connections are made between the artificial arm and certain neuromuscular endings known to control arm movements from the brain. These connections lead to amplifiers powered by small battery cells within the bionic limb. When a signal comes from the amputee's brain to, say, lower the arm, the signal is greatly amplified to actuate a small electric motor, which is geared to depress the arm at

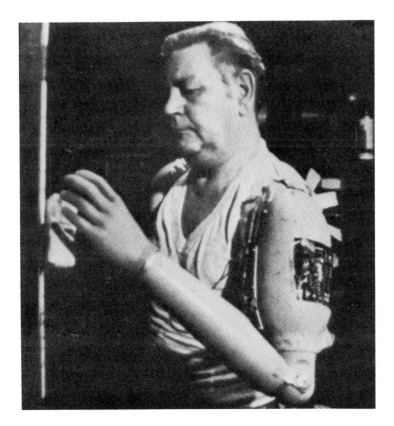

A bionic arm prosthetic device developed by the Veteran's Administration is connected to the wearer's neuromuscular system.

the elbow joint. Similar tiny motors provide movement at the wrist and a grasping action in the hand. Thus the amputee actually "thinks" his bionic arm's various movements with brain

103

power. If the arm has not moved far enough to do something, the wearer sends out more neurological impulses until it has.

Another medical application of robotics is in human organ assistance, where the devices must not only be miniaturized but very durable and reliable as well. Pacemakers are particularly good examples of such an application. Now implanted in the chests of well over 100,000 heart patients, pacemakers provide an electronically controlled pulse to help regulate their heartbeats. Specifically, this tiny robot takes over for the small patch of tissue in the heart that normally beats time for the heart muscle. Like the coxswain of a racing shell calling strokes for his oarsmen, the pacemaker signals the heart muscle when to squeeze and when to relax. If the coxswain fails to control his crew's rhythmic strokes, his shell may lose the race. Likewise, if the heart's rhythm-keeper falters and the heartbeats become abnormal, the results may be disastrous. The heart's output of pumped blood weakens or even stops.

A pacemaker is connected to the heart by wires passed into the heart, either by threading them through a vein until they reach the inner surface of the organ or by open-heart surgical techniques, whereby the wires are sewn into the heart muscle. The pacemaker itself, about the size of a small watch, is implanted under the skin near the heart. Powered by batteries that can be recharged while in use, the pacemaker consists of an incredibly tiny signal generator that sends out the correct rhythmic pulses to regulate the heartbeat. Other medical robotic mechanisms have been developed to replace damaged heart valves, to act as artificial lungs, and to analyze blood samples at great speeds.

In the space field, the launching of another un-manned satellite is no longer news. Hundreds of them are now in orbit around the earth. These faithful and efficient robots are serving human beings today in a variety of ways. The Tiros series are orbiting robot meteorologists that photograph global weather conditions and televise them back to receivers on Earth. Robot sentries of the Midas series are programed to monitor possible enemy guided missile launchings. Navigation satellites help aircraft and ships at sea to take their bearings and determine their exact positions. All kinds of communications satellites, from which telephone and television signals can be bounced from one point on the earth to another, are in daily use. Scientific orbital satellites gather and relay back to Earth valuable data about cosmic radiation, the frequency of micrometeorites, the Earth's magnetic field, and solar flares.

A typical scientific satellite performs its preprogramed job automatically. The science of measuring something in one place and reporting the results in another is called "telemetry." If a satellite is designed, say, to measure the temperature of the sun, it does so at a particular point in its orbit when it is nearest the sun. Instruments within the satellite note the temperature of the sun at this orbital point, then record this data in a number code, which is then sent earthward by a radio transmitter. For power the satellite uses both storage batteries and solar cells, which convert the sun's radiant energy into electrical current to run the transmitter.

When an antenna catches the satellite's signals on Earth, the receiving station amplifies them and records them on magnetic tape. Scientists then feed the recorded data into a computer, and the message is analyzed and translated into usable form. Aloft in space the robot satellite continues to perform this chore in orbit after orbit. Unless it is commanded to descend or its battery power somehow deteriorates, this space robot will continue at its job for decades. It has been predicted that some Midas missile detectors in 2000-mile high orbits, where no atmospheric friction can slow them down, may still be orbiting the Earth in A.D. 100,-000.

The Viking I and Viking II landers placed on Mars by the United States were the most complex robots ever constructed by human beings. They have proved remarkably dependable, and nearly all of their systems have operated according to plan as they carry out various scientific experiments on the planet. Those that failed were repairable upon radioed instructions from earth in almost every case. As with the earth-orbiting satellites, the data gathered by the two Viking landers is transmitted back to earth by telemetry.

One of the chief robotic functions of the landers is to collect soil samples from the Martian surface. For this a lander is equipped with a long arm, or boom. Like the manipulator arms of industrial robots, it has several degrees of freedom. Upon radio commands from scientists on Earth, servo-

A Viking lander robotic boom taking soil samples.

motors can sweep the boom left or right and also raise or lower it to permit sampling in different locations. At the end of the boom, a wrist capable of a twist movement is fitted with a collector head containing magnets. When the magnets are activated from Earth, they can determine by attraction whether the Martian soil contains particles with magnetic properties. When the Martian soil samples have been collected, they are funneled up through the boom by a compressed air system and deposited for analysis in one of three cylinders on the body of the lander. The data is then telemetered to scientists on Earth.

Although human astronauts were piloting the space shuttle *Columbia* during its successful flights in the early 1980s, much of the actual driving was done by robot systems. Chief among these is the automatic pilot that can keep the *Columbia* on course in space. Aircraft in the atmosphere and ships at sea all use a similar system. An automatic pilot is based upon the property of a gyroscope to point steadily in a given direction. If you take a toy gyroscope, set it spinning, and put it in any attitude on a table, its axis will point continuously in the direction in which it is set. If you put it on the rim of a glass, it remains balanced there—still pointing in the same direction. The gyroscope seems to defy gravity. Because of this unerring pointing ability, a gyroscope can be used as a compass. It is then called a gyrocompass. By pointing their axles at true north and making course adjustments as necessary, gyrocompasses can keep ships and aircraft on course. In the case of a spacecraft, the gyrocompass can be set to point continuously at the North Star, say, or another star or stars from which bearings may be taken and the craft's course corrected.

A modern automatic pilot system such as that aboard the *Columbia* consists of a series of gyrocompasses that have been robotized to keep the ship on course. Once the course is set by the astronaut, he need not stay at the controls. The automatic pilot uses photocell "eyes" that can pick up light from the stars and reflected radar beams from the moon or certain points on earth to check the craft's position in flight. A computer constantly cross-checks these data with the gyrocompasses's directional attitudes to maintain the desired course.

SIX

Robots and the Future

Surely the number of robots will increase in the future and make enormous contributions to the productivity of our society, while increasing our opportunities for leisure at the same time. By the early decades of the twenty-first century these machines, through new advances in robotics technology, will be more versatile, efficient, and a great deal "smarter."

In plants and factories particularly, industrial robots of various types will become more sophisticated and flexible in the way they carry out their tasks. New technologies are sure to bring the high price of playback robots down substantially and make them easier to install and use. As more rapid teaching methods develop, operators will no longer have to set a robot's point-sequences by hand. Sensor-aided robots that guide themselves according to information gathered about each workpiece by sensory devices like photocells are also certain to improve. Already international co-operation has produced progress in this area. Kawasaki Heavy Industries of Japan is working with Unimation, Inc. of the United States to pro-duce better sensor-aided welding robots that can interpret complex visual data.

Industrial robot makers and users look forward to the day when many plants and factories are "manless" and completely automated to produce a product. However, this degree of automation will depend largely on the successful development of practical assembly robots. Of all the jobs in a manufacturing plant, assembling a product is usually the most tedious and most difficult to au-tomate because it requires such a high degree of dexterity. Once assembly lines are so automated, unmanned factories will at last become a reality, as operatorless machining units, assembly robots, and automated transport and warehousing systems all work together to complete the entire production process.

For many manufacturing jobs, however, people will always be more efficient and less costly than robots. And for other jobs conventional production machinery will prove superior to robots. Ideally, industrial robots will be used to maximize the worth and productivity of human beings. By releasing people from the most dangerous, hot, boring, and mind-numbing tasks and allowing them to use their full human potential, robots could end up not only mechanizing production but humanizing it.

Robotized homes—ones not requiring constant attention by their owners—are a distinct possibility in the next century. Glass-domed solar houses, as seen in the accompanying photo, are already on the design boards of imaginative architects. In such a house, the round living quarters could be engineered to rotate under the dome to take advantage of the sun's energy, which can be converted to heat and electricity. Electronic robot

An artist's conception of a robot solar home of the future. Electronic robot sun-trackers would keep the house facing directly into or away from the sun as desired by the owners. The whole house would rotate under the glass dome to receive solar energy.

sun-trackers would keep the house facing directly into or away from the sun as desired by the owners. Inside this future home, other robotic devices would perform such chores as raising and lowering curtains, locking doors automatically at night, sliding doors open and shut, and switching TV channels at the command of the owner's voice.

A number of robotics engineers predict the time will come when rented or purchased radio-controlled robots will take care of household tasks like cooking, sweeping, lawn mowing, bedmaking, and even baby-sitting. Indeed, certain specialty companies offer what they call "domestic androids" right now. One such firm sells a 180-pound, five-foot-two-inch-tall Mechanical Servant which has thirty-six-inch long tubular arms with functioning elbows, wrists, and tri-pincer (three-fingered) hands.

The Mechanical Servant has an "on-board" computer that the homeowner can program with a hand-held teach pendant. The robot is charged with electrical power from a wall outlet and, once its program has been set and activated, radio commands go out in sequence to its mobile wheels and to servos in its arms and wrists. The Mechanical Servant's standard household functions include answering the door when guests arrive, announcing visitors (it has a preprogamable 250-word vocabulary), adjusting thermostats, vacuuming rugs, dusting, serving drinks and snacks on a tray, polishing floors, and monitoring the home for fire, smoke, or unauthorized intruders. The same firm offers an imposing nine-foot-tall "sentry robot" that can patrol large areas outside a house. Other firms sell or rent "sales promotional androids" similar to the Mechanical Servant that roll about, "talk," help cut ribbons, and otherwise entertain people at trade shows, sales meetings, store openings, and other functions.

Some robotics engineers even foresee that in coming decades our vehicles will be computer-robotized. For instance, there might be a portable computer control unit that a driver could plug into his or her car's steering system. The driver would punch out a destination and, with the steering system being controlled by photocell sensor eyes, the car would automatically be guided through traffic and stoplights to its destination. Similar robotic guidance systems could also be made to run

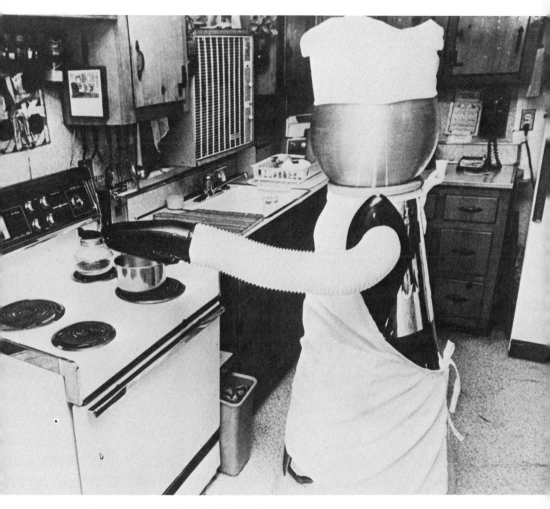

A domestic android called The Mechanical Servant now in actual use in homes. The homeowner can program the robot with a teach pendant to answer the door, dust, vacuum rugs, serve drinks, and perform other tasks.

long-haul trucking rigs, aircraft, trains, ships, and farm vehicles.

Because of the vast body of accumulated and memory-stored knowledge that will be available in future decades, information and learning centers of all kinds are certain to be robotized. Visual, voice, and print-out retrieval information units will be available to all persons concerned in libraries, classrooms, government and business offices, scientific and industrial data repositories, and in all places where knowledge is needed instantly. And because such stored information can be retrieved and beamed to points around the globe in a fraction of a second, more knowledge can be shared among people and nations.

In the medical field, vast improvements in bionic limbs and organ-assisting and replacement devices are sure to come. There is also serious speculation among doctors about the possibility that delicate feedback between an ultra-sensitive computer control unit and the human brain might produce information that would help in mental health. By means of such monitoring, they say, thinking patterns leading to mental breakdowns could be predicted and steps could be taken to avoid them. A few hospitals have successfully employed home robots of the Mechanical Servant kind to assist nurses in caring for handicapped and bedridden patients. The robots serve meals, take temperatures, vacuum rooms, and are even programed to make "small talk" to keep up a patient's spirits. Quite likely more will be so used in the future to free nurses for more important jobs.

As further advances in space technology are made, new and improved robotics will be in the forefront. In addition to the more accurate automatic gyropilots that will be designed, greater use will be made of robots as monitors, backup systems, and maintenance devices. On NASA's drawing boards right now is a concept for a Maneuvering Work Platform, known unofficially as Space Horse. Developed to help astronauts work in space outside their vehicles, Space Horse will have three double-jointed arms with grippers at their wrists, which will make manipulating jobs simpler in weightless conditions. Some space experts are predicting that, on routine space missions at least, robots will be replacing astronauts altogether. For in fact, robots are less trouble and more efficient than people in space situations.

ROBOTICS

They do not have to be provided with elaborate life-support systems and other paraphernalia required by human beings.

Whether we look upon robots with favor or suspicion, they have become just as much a part of our world as space flight, color television, and the threat of nuclear war. The best that we may hope for them is that, far from becoming our masters as they did in the fictional *R.U.R.*, they will share our world as helpful partners in human progress.

A nine-foot-tall "Robot Sentry Guard" can patrol large areas outside a house to frighten away intruders.

Index

italic indicates illustration

121

INDEX